Beauty with a Birthmark

Written by
Erica Maxwell
and
Jessica A. Alexander

Illustrated by
Awele Emili

BEAUTY WITH A BIRTHMARK
Published by:
Bubbles Publishing
Email: erica.alexander0104@gmail.com

Erica Maxwell, Publisher
Yvonne Rose/Quality Press.info, Book Packager
Illustrator: Awele Emili

ALL RIGHTS RESERVED

No part of this book may be reproduced or transmitted in any form or by any means electronic or mechanical, including photocopying, recording or by any information storage and retrieval system without written permission from the author, except for the inclusion of brief quotations in a review.

Copyright ©2021 by Erica Maxwell and Jessica A. Alexander
ISBN #: 978-1-7372388-0-5
Library of Congress Control Number: 2021917142

To Bubbs,

You are my beauty with a birthmark! Love you ∞
—E.M.

I will praise thee; for I am fearfully and wonderfully made

Psalm 139:14 (KJV)

I am a beauty with a birthmark
on the right side of my face.

Had it since I was born and it's
in the same exact place.

My birthmark travels with me everywhere that I go.

It's a special part of me, just like my fingers and my toes.

We have been to school, piano, Girl Scouts, cheer, and track.

My birthmark is something that I would never give back.

We live in Arizona also known as Out West.

Visiting family across the country is simply the best!

I am a beauty with a birthmark on my mocha colored skin.

And my birthmark and I have made some very good friends.

They are supportive, fun, and a part of many things that I do.

True friends will accept your birthmark as a part of being you!

I am a beauty with a birthmark
that started out being dark green.

Black, brown, red, and purple
are birthmark colors I have seen.

I am a beauty with a birthmark with an interesting name.

My dermatologist, or skin doctor, took the time to explain.

There are many types of birthmarks so I'll just name a few.

Some people have one and many have more than two.

One type of birthmark is called a salmon patch.

Birthmarks are not like a cold, they're not something you can catch.

Salmon patches on the back of the neck are called stork bites.

They may fade away with time, they might disappear from sight!

Angel kisses are salmon patches located on the face.

Birthmarks make you special, because you cannot be replaced.

My birthmark is Nevus of Ota and does not cause me any pain.

Other types of birthmarks can be Mongolian spots and port wine stains.

I am a beauty with a birthmark which gives me a very distinct look.

One day I'll rock the runway and grace the cover of a magazine or book.

Everyone has a mark, maybe a scar, freckles, or a mole.

What matters most of all is the beauty deep down in your soul.

You are a beauty who may have a mark located on your skin.

It's beautiful on the outside, but true beauty comes from within.

GLOSSARY

Freckles
A group of brown spots found on the face most of the time.

Moles
Brown or black spot that can be found anywhere on the body which can change in size and color as children grow older.

Mongolian Spots
A flat, dark area that is blue-green or closer to black and may look like a bruise on the back or butt. It may disappear as children grow older.

Nevus of Ota

A dark area on the face and around the eye that is blue or brown in color. It may also be a dark spot on the white portion of the eye.

Port Wine Stains

Pink or purple birthmark that is permanent and often changes color as children grow older.

Salmon Patch

Pink or reddish patches found on the back of the neck, eyelids, or between the eyes. They sometimes disappear as children grow older. Also known as stork bites and angel kisses.

ABOUT THE AUTHORS

Erica Maxwell is the proud mother of Jessica and Ronald. In addition to being a first time author, she is an active member of the Chandler, AZ community. With over 25 years of experience as an educator, Erica served as the first ever associate superintendent of equity, diversity, and inclusion for Arizona's Department of Education.

Jessica A. Alexander is a beauty with a birthmark and the main character in the book. She is an active teenager who enjoys time with family and friends while balancing academics and work. Jessica is looking forward to attending a Historically Black College or University (HBCU) to pursue a career in psychology.

ABOUT THE ILLUSTRATOR

Awele Emili is an award-winning illustrator, animator and pharmacologist. She has partnered with various brands such as Facebook Inc. to create amazing artworks for books. She uses her love for art to bring stories to life!

www.ingramcontent.com/pod-product-compliance
Lightning Source LLC
Chambersburg PA
CBHW051259110526
44589CB00025B/2888